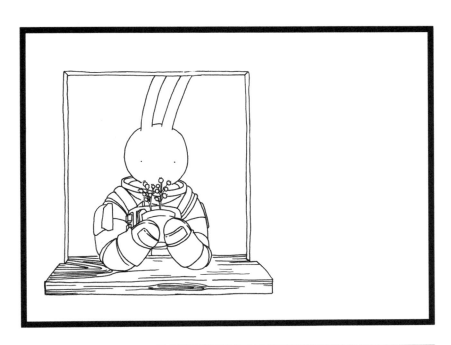

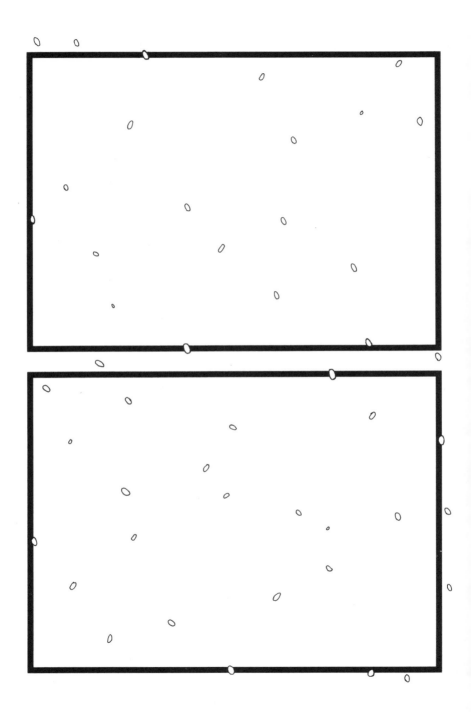

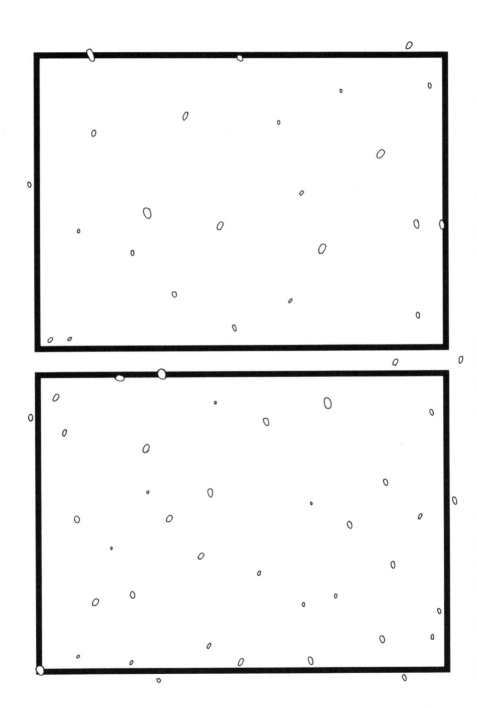

THE GORGEOUS HABOUR

LE PORT MAGNIFIQUE

à mr clement comic

une bande dessinée de mr clément

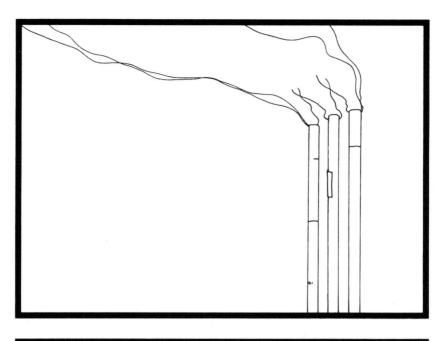

"Why did they build the factory here?"
"Pourquoi ont-ils construit cette usine ici?"

"I think... it's for our city's future."
"À mon avis... c'est pour l'avenir de notre ville."

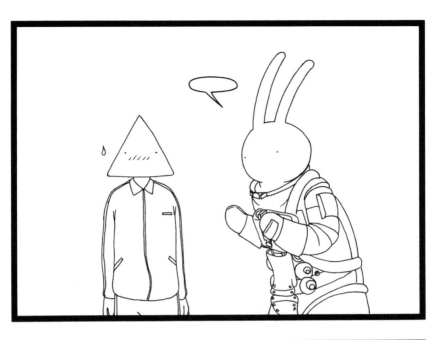

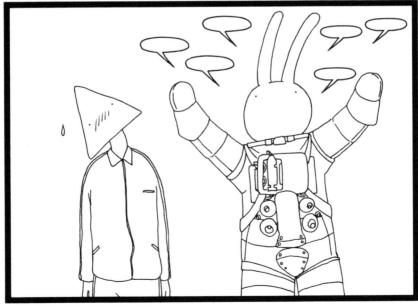

"Okay, but how about the harbour's future?
The landscape's future?
Your son's future?
How about our future?"
"D'accord, mais que va-t-il advenir du port?
Du paysage?
De ton fils?
De notre avenir?"

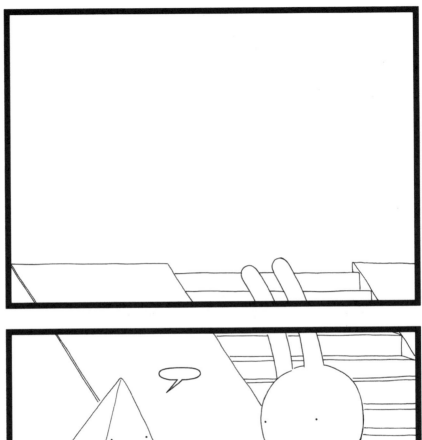

"You can leave again if you aren't happy."
"Tu peux repartir si t'es pas content."

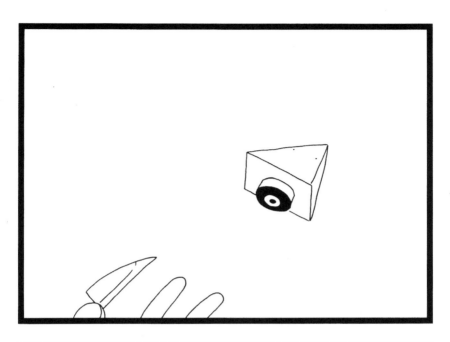

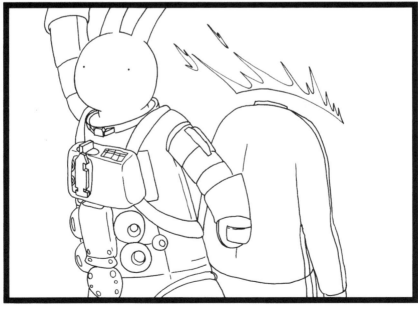

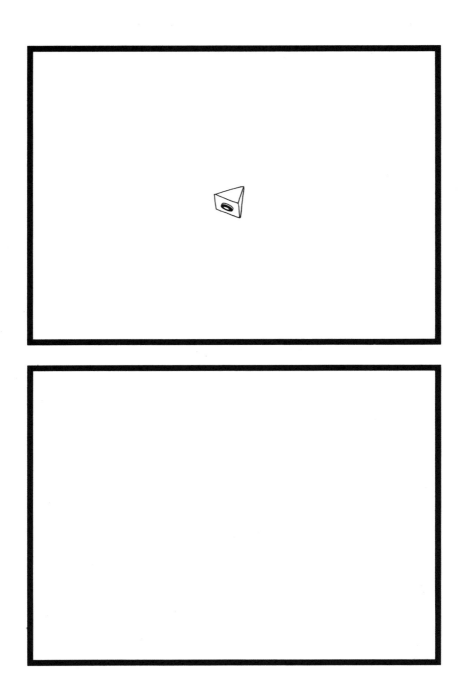

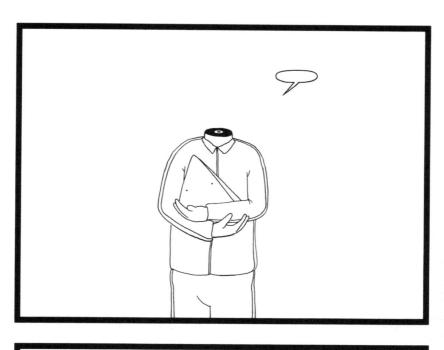

"Where are you going?... Will you come back?"
"Où vas-tu?... Vas-tu revenir?"

"One day...soon..."
"Un de ces jours...bientôt..."

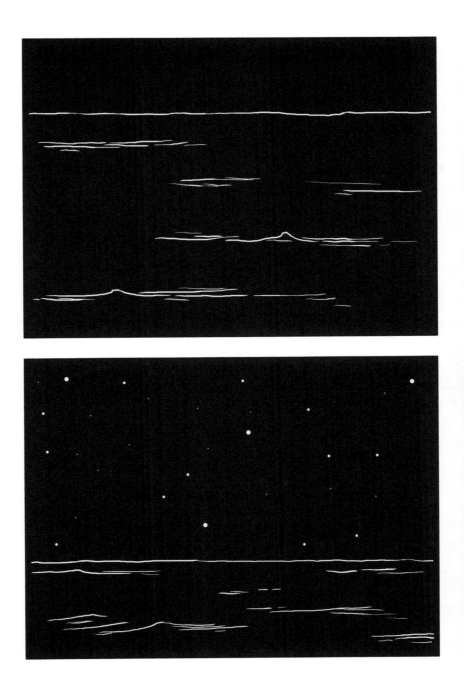

"Oh! It's lovely!!!"
"Oh! C'est joli!!!"

"Oh! It's gorgeous!!!"
"Oh! C'est magnifique!!!"

"Oh! My neck hurts!!!"
"Oh! J'ai mal au cou!!!"

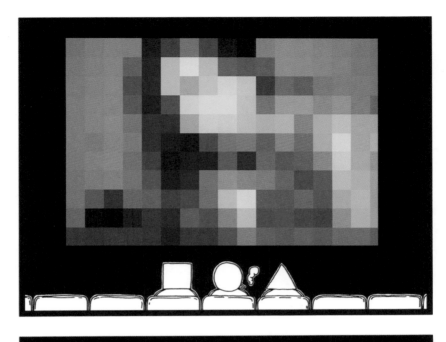

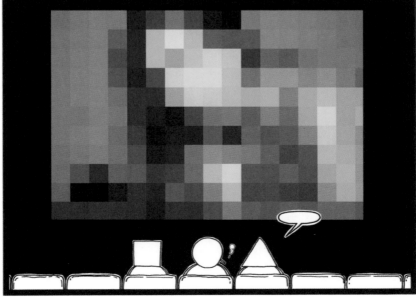

"Oh! It's lovely!!!"
"Oh! C'est joli!!!"

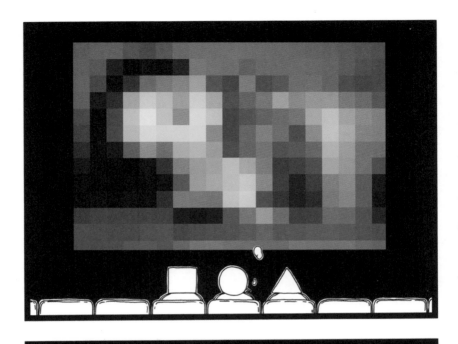

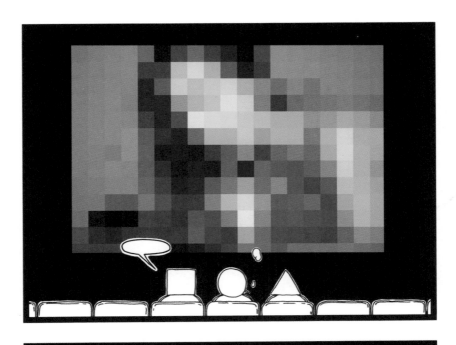

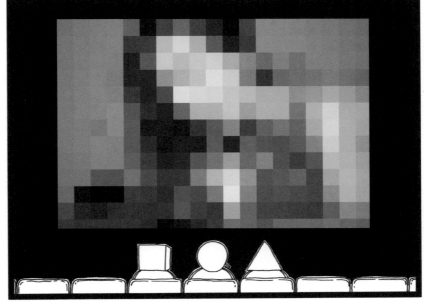

"Oh! It's gorgeous!!!"
"Oh! C'est magnifique!!!"

"Oh! Her neck hurts!!!"
"Oh! Elle a mal au cou!!!"

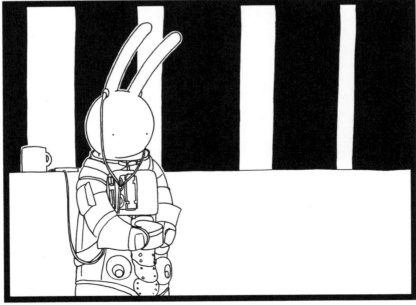

"What is it?"
"Qu'est-ce que c'est?"

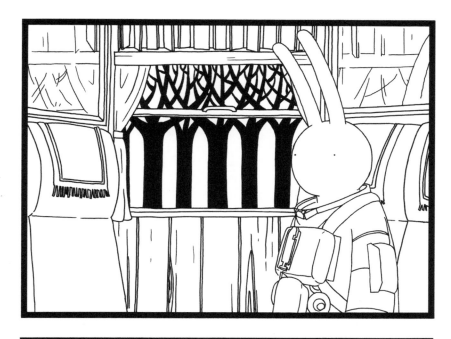

He appeared in front of me.
Il est apparu devant moi.

He looked at me.
Il m'a regardé.

He seemed to be looking at me...
Il paraissait me regarder...

.... he seemed to be looking at me.
.... il paraissait me regarder.

"Where will you go?"
I asked him before he left the train.
"Où vas-tu aller?"
Lui ai-je demandé avant qu'il descende du train.

He took a photo from his pocket to show it to me.
Il a sorti une photo de sa poche pour me la montrer.

I didn't say anything. That factory had been destroyed in a summer, because the islanders didn't like the idea of having it in their place.

Je n'ai rien dit. Cette usine avait été détruite un été, parce que les habitants n'aimaient pas avoir cela sur leur île.

It was the first time we met and separated.

C'était la première fois que l'on se rencontrait et séparait.

"I ---e you."
"Je t'---e."

"What?" "I ---e you."
"Quoi?" "Je t'---e."

"I ---e you, I ---e you, I ---e you,
I ---e you...!!!"
"Je t'---e, Je t'---e, Je t'---e,
Je t'---e...!!!"

"You never know whether he loves you, or not. Hahaha..."
"Tu ne sais jamais s'il t'aime ou non. Hahaha..."

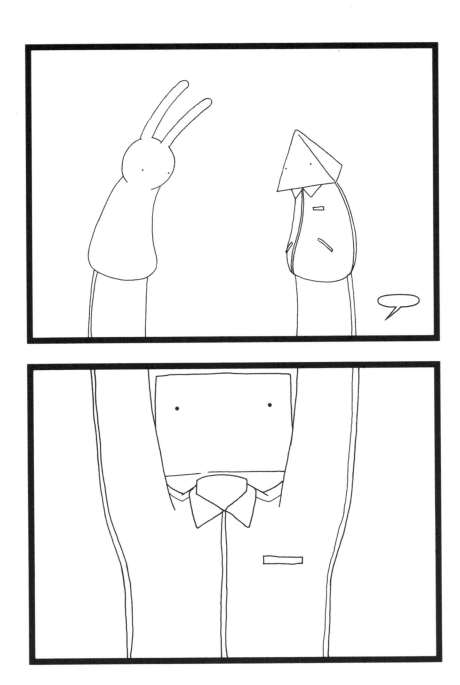

"You never know whether he loves you, or not.
Hahaha..."
"Tu ne sais jamais s'il t'aime ou non.
Hahaha..."

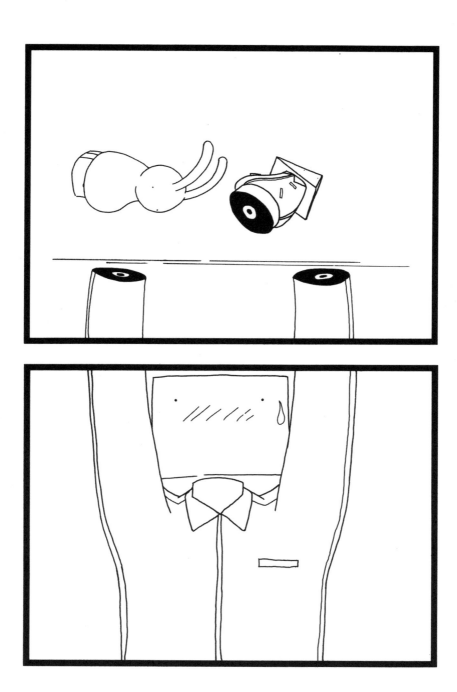

"Don't think you can have him before I die..."
"Ne pense pas que tu puisses l'avoir avant que je meure..."

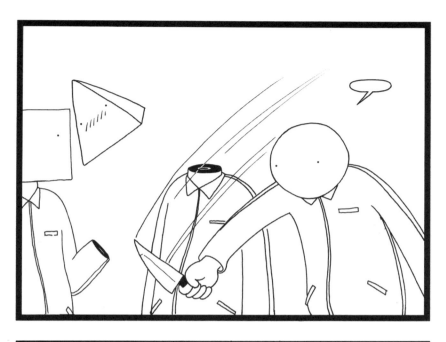

"Don't think you can have him before I die..."
"Ne pense pas que tu puisses l'avoir avant que je meure..."

"You too!!!"
"Toi aussi!!!"

" I don't care how far I need to go,
if I could live with you."
"Cela m'est bien égal d'avoir à aller loin,
si je pouvais vivre avec toi."

"I don't care what you care, but you should know this frame is too small for me or for us."
"Je m'en fiche de ce que tu penses, mais tu dois te rendre compte que ce cadre est trop petit pour moi ou pour nous."

"I don't care how small this frame is, if I could live with you."

"Je m'en fiche de la dimension du cadre, si je pouvais vivre avec toi."

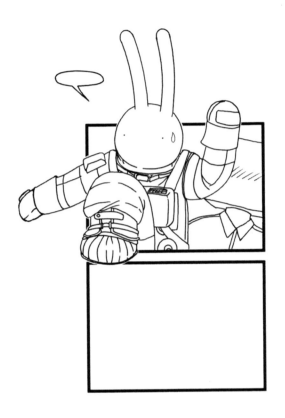

"Shit!!"
"Merde!!"

"Where are you going, my astrolapin?"
"Où vas-tu, mon petit astrolapin?"

"Where are you going?"
"Où vas-tu?"

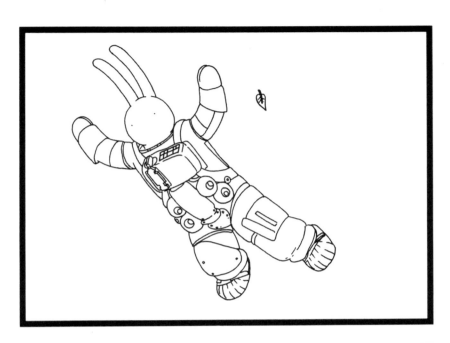

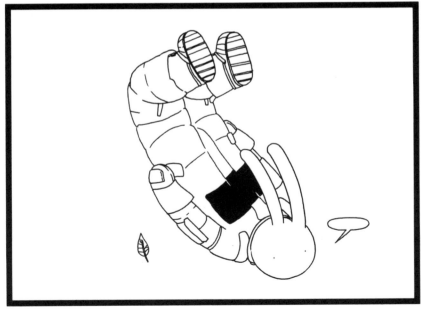

"O! it's great... I can fly..."
"O! c'est formidable... Je peux voler..."

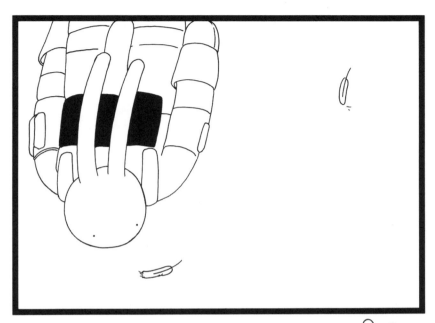

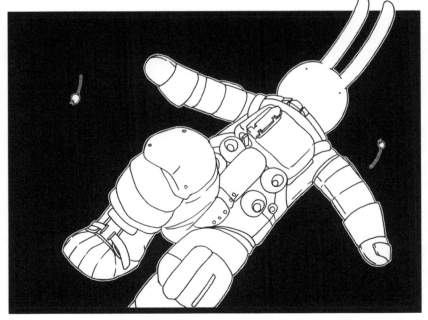

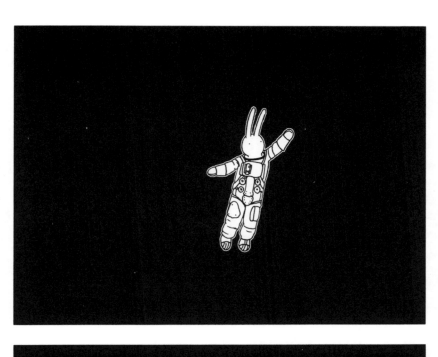

intermission

intermission

intermission

intermission

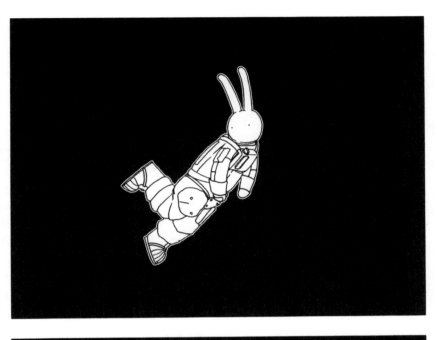

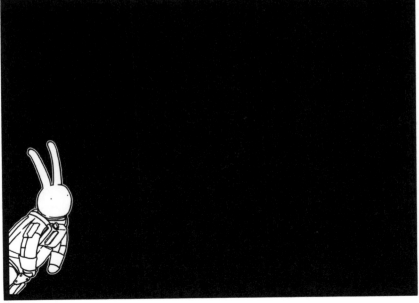

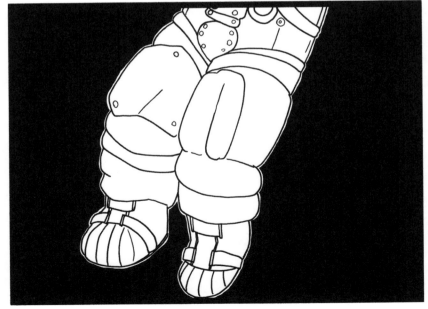

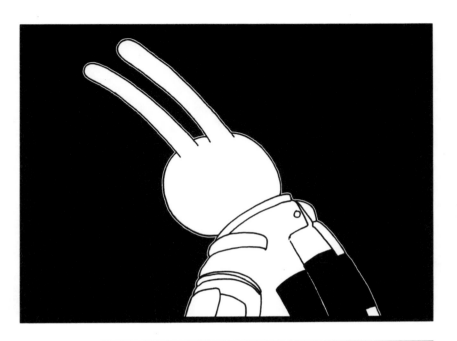

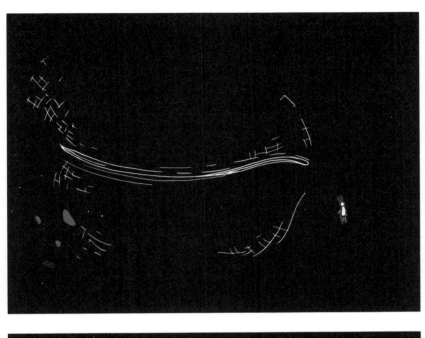

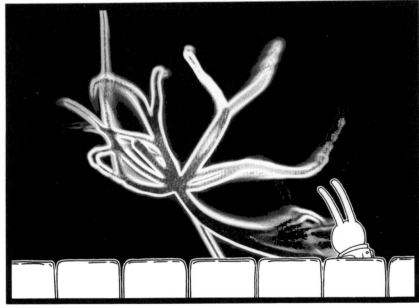

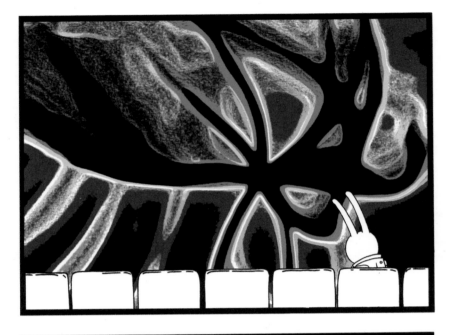

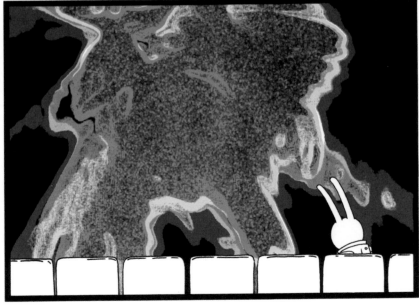

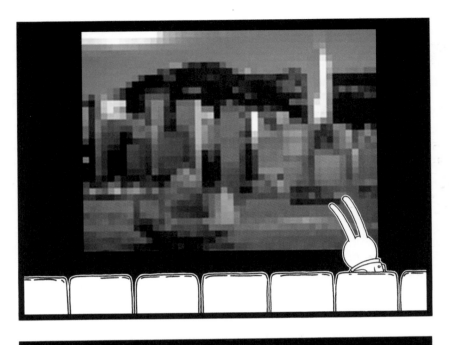

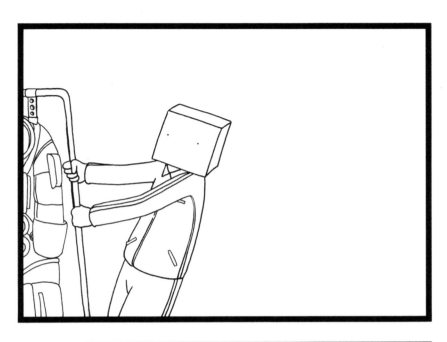

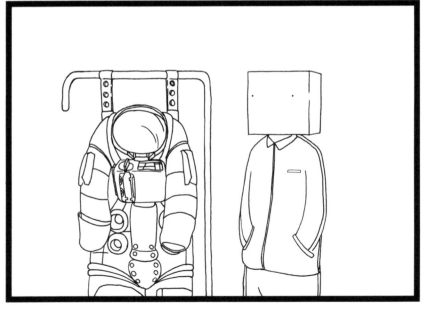

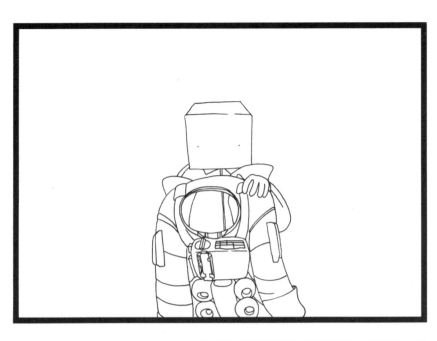

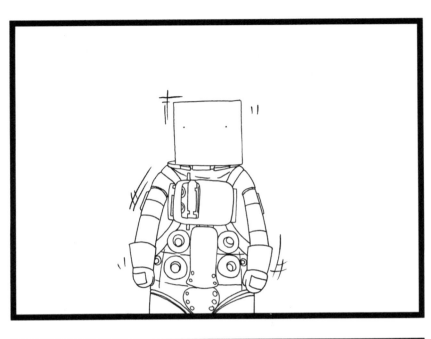

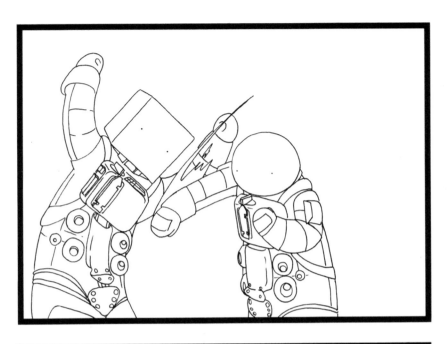

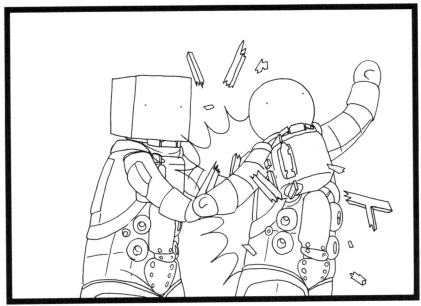

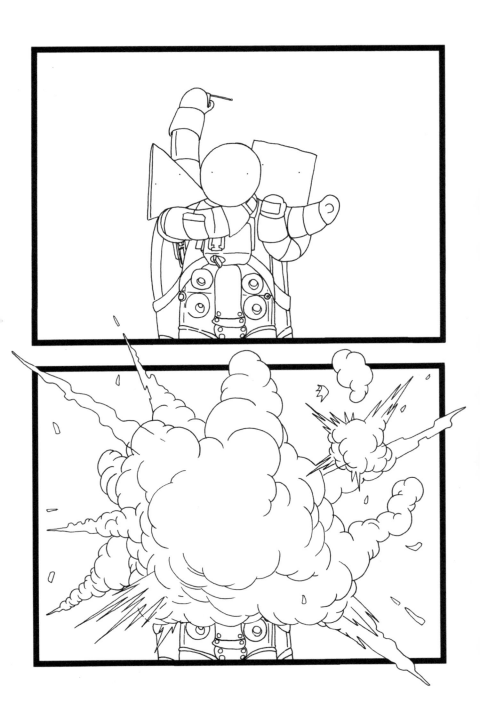

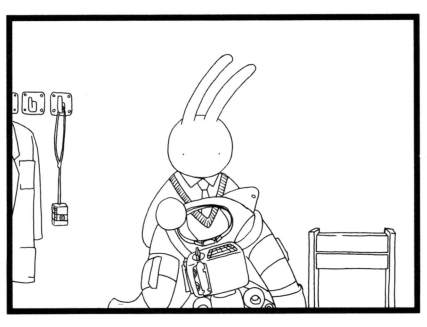

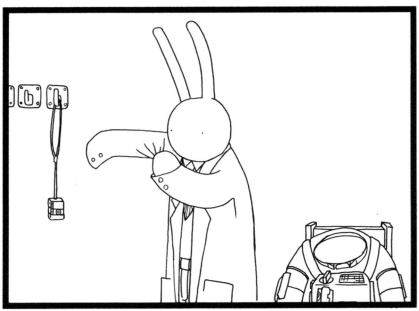

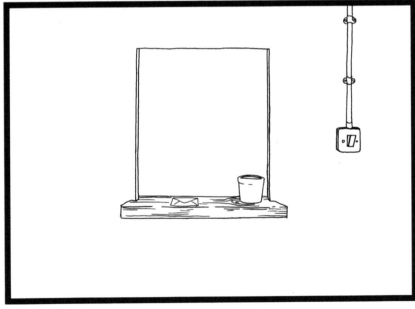

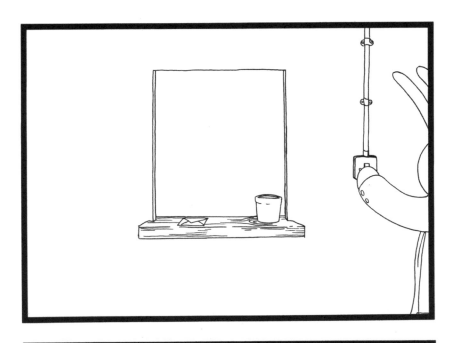

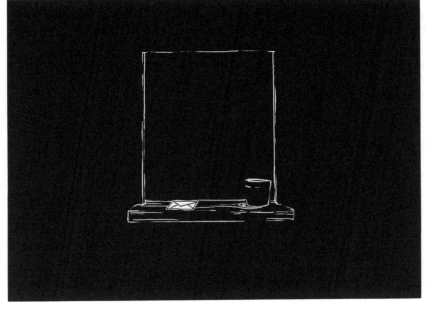

This is a story of Love and Places.
C'est une petite histoire d'amour et de lieux.

mr clement

END

FIN

This collection first published in 2004 by
Première publication de ce livre en l'an 2004 par

a rewind records production

Distributed by
Distribué par

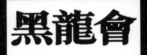

Black Dragon Production
6/F 23 Queen's Road East, Wan Chai, Hong Kong
Tel.no: (852) 21049706
E-mail: black_dragon_hk@hotmail.com

Author
Auteur
mr clement

Editor-in-Chief
Sous la direction de
dj luka

Graphic Designer
Conception graphique
bear

Consultant
Conseiller
Yip Ching Ho

English Translator
Traductrice pour l'Anglais

jenny lampstand

French Translator
Traductrice pour le Français

Nicole Sicard

www.mrclement.com

Supported by

香港藝術發展局
Hong Kong Arts Development Council

The judgement and opinions expressed and
the content included in this publication do not carry
technical endorsement or authentication by,
nor necessarily represent the views of the Hong
Kong Arts Development Council.

Printed in Hong Kong, China by
Imprimé à Hong Kong, Chine par

Hang Sing Printing & Design Company
15/F, Blk. E & F, Derrick Industrial Bldg.,
49-51, Wong Chuk Hang Rd., Hong Kong
tel. (852)25546311 fax (852)28733335

ISBN 988-97778-1-9